CW00865727

Why Should I Forgive

Why Should I Forgive

By Travis W. Simmons

XULON PRESS

Xulon Press
2301 Lucien Way #415
Maitland, FL 32751
407.339.4217
www.xulonpress.com

Unless otherwise indicated, Scripture quotations taken from the Holy Bible, New Living Translation (NLT). Copyright ©1996, 2004, 2007 by Tyndale House Foundation. Used by permission of Tyndale House Publishers, Inc.

Printed in the United States of America.

ISBN-13: 978-1-6312-9187-6

In this book I will explain how you can equip yourself to be able to completely forgive everyone that has wronged you.

Nothing is impossible, just look what God gave up for us!

Table of Contents

Why Should I Forgive?

One of the greatest factors in life to gain success spiritually is forgiveness. As we all know, Jesus gave His life for us so we could repent for our sins and find forgiveness in Him, that we may have eternal life with Him in heaven. Forgiveness first started with Him. God gave us His son so that we may have a chance to

1

have eternal life in Heaven and not perish in hell. John 3:16 *"For God so loved the world that he gave his only Son, that whoever believes in him should not perish but have eternal life."* If we believe in Jesus, then we believe in forgiveness. I know it is easier said than done and depending on what has been done to us, how can we forgive that person who has wronged us? I used to have that mindset until Jesus "broke" me free from that bondage. I had to study the word and dig deep inside myself and find out why it was so hard for me to forgive. Even when I thought I was forgiving someone, I really wasn't. Now I'm sure you are asking, "what does he mean by that"?

Well in my psyche, I would keep bringing up what that person did to me, or I could not be around them without feeling a certain way which was destroying me inside and hindering my relationship with God. In this book I will explain how you can equip yourself to be able to completely forgive any and everyone that has wrong you. Nothing is impossible, just look what God gave up for us!

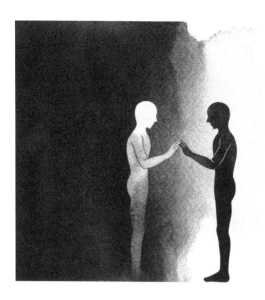

The Flesh Verse the Spirit

Sometimes we get caught up in life and forget that this life is not our permanent home. When we leave this world there are only two places that we can go, Heaven or Hell. I choose to go to Heaven to be with my Heavenly Father, but in order to do so, we must prepare ourselves and equip ourselves spiritually by living as "Christ-like" as possible while on this earth. When Christ was being wrongly crucified, he asked God in Luke 23:34, *"Father, forgive them, for they know not what they do."* Many of us would think that it would be impossible for us to forgive them like Christ did and it would be, if we were trying to forgive through our flesh but everything Christ did was through the Spirit. What we must understand is that, as Christians through the spirit and through Christ, all things are possible. Our bodies are only temples of our true selves (The Holy Spirit) that abides in.

The enemy tries to confuse us of this. Ephesians 6:12 states, *"For we do not wrestle against flesh and blood, but against the rulers, against the authorities, against the cosmic powers over this present darkness, against the spiritual forces of evil in the heavenly places."* This is why we must strive to walk by the spirit and not by the flesh. Our Flesh will always try to tempt us to sin. That is the nature of the flesh. Our Flesh are vessels and sometimes we go into "auto pilot" and let our vessels steer themselves. We have to change that process.

Our spirit must guide our vessel at all times by following the "flight plan" which is outlined in the Bible. We must always be on alert to be able to weather all storms that will come our way. Once we give our lives to Christ, we belong to him and the only way that the devil can get to us is by temping our flesh.

What people tend to fail at is that they only see what their eyes see and not what their heart and spirits sees. Hebrews 11:1 says *"Now faith is assurance of things hoped for, a conviction of things not seen."* The flesh only sees what's in this world, but living by faith, our spirit shows us how to survive this earthly world and prepare us for our eternal life. John 6:47 also states *"Verily, verily, I say unto you, He that Believeth Hath eternal Life."*

A friend once told me that we live to die. I took it as everyone will eventually die, because no one lives forever, but what he meant was that what we sow now, we will reap in eternal life. If you don't give your life to Christ and continue to allow your flesh to control you, then you will be cast in the eternal fire of hell when you leave this earth. If you give your life to Christ and have faith, follow His word, and seek Him first then you will inherit enteral life with Him.

Jesus is in us and he loves us! Ask him for help to conquer your flesh and he will provide a pathway for you. 1 Corinthians 10: 13 says *"The temptations in your life are no different from what others experience. And God is faithful. He will not allow the temptation to be more than you can stand. When you are tempted, he will show you a way out so that you can endure."* Remember that if what you are doing, is not of the word, then it is of the flesh and you will need to repent! If you don't know what you are doing falls in line with the word, then you will need to pray and read your Bible. It will show you in detail how to live for Christ Jesus our Lord.

Forgiving Yourself

O ne of the hardest things that people do not realize is some times it is difficult to forgive yourself. We miss out on so many blessings because we are not able to move forward from our past. If we repent Jesus said that he forgives us. Acts 3:19 reads *"Now repent of your sins and turn to God, so that your*

sins may be wiped away." Our Lord is stating that if you repent, then He forgives us; He wipes away your sin, so why do we not forgive ourselves? This is another strategy from the devil. Forgiveness is another gift from the Lord and what the devil tries to do is to strip us of that gift by bringing up our past.

We all have sinned and have fallen short from the glory of God, but that is why he sent his son Jesus to die for our sins, so that we can be forgiven and have eternal life with Him. Forgive yourself! God has and the devil can't stand that.

God loves us and we all make mistakes! We must repent, ask for forgiveness, and learn from them. When the devil tries to bring your past up again, start praying to God, ask Him for strength to rebuke the devil. Find peace in His word and know that it is ok to forgive yourself, no matter what the situation was, God forgives you, so it is ok to forgive yourself. Not forgiving yourself can bring on a lot of unnecessary stress which can cause health issues if not careful.

Stress is a state of mental or emotional strain or tension resulting from adverse or very demanding circumstances. The devil tries to destroy your mind by sending negative thoughts such as, how can God forgive you and how can I forgive myself for what I have done? When that thought comes to your mind pray and know that God is with you. Second, God stated in his word that He will forgive you as long as you repent. Also remember that God can't lie. If he said He will do it, then He will. Third, if God forgives you, then forgive yourself.

The only thing that can hold you back is you. God has given us power and we need to start using it. Just think about this. Those of us who have children. When our children make mistakes, we forgive them. Our love doesn't stop for them because they made a mistake. We don't turn our back on them. We correct them and encourage them to strive to do better. That is what our God does for us. He doesn't turn His back on us. He loves us too much.

Learn to Love Yourself as God Loves You.

Psalms 117: 2 says *"For his unfailing love for us is powerful; the Lord's faithfulness endures forever. Praise the Lord."* I encourage you to pray this prayer: *"Lord thank you for all that you are. Thank you*

for always being faithful to me when I was not always faithful to you. I give you all the praise and glory. Lord I repent for the sins that I knowingly and unknowingly have done. Please search my heart, my soul and remove all that is not of you. Please encourage me to walk by faith and to turn to you always. Lord please teach me to love myself and to forgive myself. The enemy wants me to believe that what I have done in the past is too horrible for your forgiveness, but I know that is a lie that the enemy wants me to believe. You said in your word that you will forgive me for all of my sins as long as I repent. Now Lord teach me how to forgive myself. In this prayer I ask this in Jesus name Amen. You will start seeing God work in your life.

Forgiveness is fruit for the soul. Remember that you have to stay strong in the word to be able to fight a good fight. Many people sometimes don't know how to use the word of God to fight the battle against Satan and his demons. You have to study the word and use scriptures that fits the situation that you are going through.

For example, my biggest problem was anger and frustration when things did not go my way. I would pick up the Bible and just start reading. Even though I felt a little better after reading a little, it did not completely fix my issue because I wasn't applying the right scripture to my situation. I was searching YouTube one day trying to learn ways to meditate, when I came across a pastor stating that you need to find a scripture concerning what problems you are presently going through and meditate on it.

So, I found a few scriptures. The first one was in Ephesians 4:26 that reads *"Don't sin by letting anger control you. Don't let the sun go down while you are still angry."* The second one is from James 1:20 that reads, *"Human anger does not produce the righteousness God desires."* And the third one was in the book of Matthew 5:22, which reads, *"But I say, if you are even angry with someone, you are subject to judgment! If you call someone an idiot, you are in danger of being brought before the court. And if you curse someone, you are in danger of the fires of hell."*

These scriptures helped me to overcome most of my issues.

Now I still get angry sometimes, but I immediately turn to Jesus for repentance and forgiveness and ask Him to help me overcome it. I no longer act or react to anger. By God's grace He is helping me to completely overcome my issues. He has picked me up when I have fallen and dusted me off and said, "let's try again". Don't stop and don't give up until you pass the test. Having faith in God and knowing that he has faith in you will help you move mountains. When you pray, try adding the scriptures that fits your situation into your pray and watch what happens.

You will start to feel a calmness come over you and you will have peace. That is Jesus working out your issues for you. He will deliver you from them if you ask with an open and clear heart. He wants to help you!

Forgiving others

As we go through this temporary life here on earth, we will endure pain and struggles. Some of these pains may be cause by ourselves and some may be cause by other people. How will you react when someone hurts you?

In June of 2015, my wife (Juanita) and I went to Las Vegas Nevada to celebrate our fifth-year wedding anniversary. Our daughter who was four and our son who was 17 at the time, went to their grandmother's (my wife's mother's home) in Charleston, South Carolina. Juanita and I had just settled in at the hotel when she received a call from her cousin stating that there had been a shooting in Charleston and was asking if her mother was ok. Immediately my wife called her mother to check to see if she was in fact ok; she was.

On June 17, 2015 during a prayer service at Emanuel African Methodist Episcopal Church , white supremacist Dylan Roof came to the church and subsequently killed nine church members, all African Americans, including senior pastor and state senator Clementa C. Pinckney, and injured one other person. This is the church that my wife's cousin is a member of.

Earlier that day, my mother in law's cousin, Ethel Lance stopped by to say hello and had asked if she was going to Bible study with her. My mother in law decided that she was not going to go because she had the grandkids with her. When my wife spoke to her and found that out, both of our hearts sank.

Even though it effected our family, it could have been worse if she had gone. When they finally caught the suspect, and he appeared for his arraignment, my wife's cousin Nadine, spoke and expressed to the suspect that she had forgiven him for murdering her mother.

My mouth just dropped. I was thinking how in the world could she just forgive this person for murdering her mother and it has only been little over a month? It was the grace of God in her heart. Cousin Nadine was not reacting through the flesh, she was reacting through the Holy Spirit. It took me awhile to process it, but I finally realized that everything that we all go through is a spiritual fight.

It's hard to get to that point by yourself without our Lord and Savior Jesus Christ, because from the moment when we are born, we are taught or at least most of us are taught, how to live life by the flesh. We are taught what the importance is of the world and not what the importance is of our soul. Yes, we may go to church two or three times a week for about two or three hours, but school is five times a week with six to seven-hour days, learning about who found America, the "Big Bang Theory", and a lot of other teachings that has our mind focused on the "earthly world". When your mind is trained a certain way, it's hard to un-train it and to train a different way.

That's why when one may for example join the military you first go through bootcamp to break you of your normal routine and train you in a way that the military wants you to function. That's what we have to do when we accept Jesus Christ as our Lord and Savior. We don't continue life as we lived before, we change our way of living. We must go to bootcamp, meaning studying the Bible and using it as a guide and roadmap on how we should carry ourselves and treat others. Jesus is our captain and He always leads us the right way.

Being able to see what Jesus was doing in Cousin Nadine's life made me want to have that same peace in my life. So, I prayed to Jesus and asked him to deliver me from all the anger and hate that I had in my heart from people that had done me wrong in the past.

This story that I'm about to tell you is my testimony on how Christ delivered me from the pain I had inside and showed me how to forgive others.

I was raised in a good family, both on my mother and father's side. Even though my parents were divorced, both sides of my family were all about family, meaning being there for each other and having family functions where everyone would get together. When I was a teen, one of my family members met someone and became involved and eventually they got married. The person that they married was very controlling and was physical and mentally abusive. The family member did not come around the family and when I had my first two kids out of wedlock, she refused to be around them and claimed that because I had kids did not make them her family. That devastated me so bad that I was plotting to do physical harm to her husband. By the grace of God, He gave me enough strength not to follow through on my initial ill-conceived plan, but the pain and anger inside controlled my spirit. My spirit was broken. I was a big family person and it seemed to me that my family was being broken up by this person and I could not do anything about it.

This lasted for years until I witnessed the power of forgiveness that Jesus gave Cousin Ethel. I prayed like I never prayed before asking God to turn my situation around and teach me how to forgive that family member and her husband. Well I can say Jesus answered my prayers. They divorced but they are still seeing each other. I forgave him for the abuse that he caused to the family and I forgave her for abandoning her family.

Now are you wondering if I have truly forgiven them both? The answer is a resounding yes! They both come over for family functions at my home and she comes and picks up the kids sometimes to go to eat or to a movie. You see Jesus did not just answer my prayers by helping me forgive, He went the extra mile and changed that family members' heart. Now she accepts the children and loves spending time with them. Won't He do it!

Forgiveness is the key to everything. Jesus gave up His life for us so we could be forgiven for all our sins if we repent.

It is a must that you search your heart and pray to Jesus that He provides you the power to forgive. As I mention before that some of us may believe that we have forgiven, but we really haven't.

I have placed together a list below to determine if you have truly forgiven that individual that may have wronged you at some point in your life:

- Keep bringing up the situation that offended you?
- Speaking negative about that individual?
- Can't be around that individual that wronged you?
- Spreading rumors about that individual?
- Can't speak to that individual when you see them?
- Avoiding that individual at all cost?
- Dwelling on what the individual did to offend you?

If you fall under any of the categories that I have listed above, then you have not truly forgiven that individual or individuals, that may have wronged you and you would need to pray to God to help you to completely forgive that individual. Colossians 3 states, *"Make allowance for each other's faults, and forgive anyone who offends you. Remember, the Lord forgave you, so you must forgive others."*

First **Make Allowance** means to take mitigating factors or circumstances into consideration- to pardon-excuse. Not making excuses for what that individual has done to you but there is always a bigger picture involve with all situations, and the main force that is driving everything is coming from the spiritual realm. Matthew 18:21-22 states, "*Then Peter came to him and asked, "Lord, how often should I forgive someone who sins against me? Seven times? "No, not seven times,"* *Jesus replied, "but seventy times seven".*

Remember that forgiveness is the main reason that Jesus came to this earth to lay down his life, so that God our Father could forgive us, and we can have ever lasting life. If we don't forgive, then our Heavenly Father will not forgive us.

Loving Your Enemies

The most difficult thing to do is loving your enemies. How can you love someone that has offended you or has tried everything in their power to make your life miserable or your love one's life miserable? Remember what I mentioned in the earlier part of the book. We are fighting against spirits in the heavenly realms.

God created all of us in his image and he has given everyone the chance to repent and turn to him. Luke 6:27 states, *"But I say unto you that hear, love your enemies, do good to them that hate you."* God is clearly giving us instructions to treat our enemies with love. I'm sure you are asking how do I do that. 2 Timothy 1:7 states, *"For God gave us not a spirit of fearfulness: but a power and love and discipline."* Through Jesus Christ, God has given us power and love. It is our choice if we choose to use it or not.

None of us here on earth are perfect. No matter if you are saved or not, we all sin and have to turn to God and ask for forgiveness on a daily basis. Whether we commit a sin physically or mentally, to God a sin is a sin no matter what type of sin it is. Many of us strive to be like Jesus but do not want to fight through difficult situations like He did. Jesus still showed love to those who crucified Him on the cross by asking God to forgive them. Jesus wants us to show that same love to our enemies as He did. Just think of it this way, when we sin, we are disregarding what Jesus did for us on the cross but He still loves us enough to let us come back to Him and ask for forgiveness and still will have the same relationship with us that He had before.

I have heard people say that "I can forgive but I don't have to be around that person." What if Jesus was the same way? What would happen to us if He did forgive us but did not want to have a relationship with us? We would not know what to do.

You think times are hard now, what would it be like to have Jesus completely remove himself out of your life? I would not want to find out how that would feel.

We as Christians also must realize that what ever the situation that is causing us not to love our enemies, we are unconsciously judging that person for their sin! Matthew 7:1-5 states, *"Do not judge others, and you will not be judged. For you will be treated as you treat others. The standard you use in judging is the standard by which you will be judged. And why worry about a speck in your friend's eye when you have a log in your own? How can you think of saying to your friend, let me help you get rid of that speck in your eye, when you can't see past the log in your own eye? Hypocrite! First get rid of the log in your own eye; then you will see well enough to deal with the speck in your friend's eye."*

My pastor once said if you just see a person for who they are physically, then you don't have any vision.

You must look past what they are in the flesh and have vision on what they could be spiritually in the future.

God forgave Paul which his name was Saul at the time for killing and arresting anyone who followed Jesus. He even went the extra mile and used Paul to spread the good news around and win over souls for the Kingdom of God. Again, I know it's easier said than done, but if you have vision instead of site, meaning if you have faith that it can happen and you can see it happening without relying on your physical site, then it will. Having faith and vision is seeing things spiritual and not seeing things physically , that's why God sent His son to give up His life because God who is faith had vision that we could be better than we are now if given the chance.

We must look deep into our hearts and truly search why we can't forgive and learn to love our Enemies and ask God to remove that so we can learn to love all people good or bad.

What if everyone knew your dark most inner secrets, would they still look at you the same?

We are in a spiritual warfare and we need to realize it so we can win the battle. Some may say God is still working on me, but it must come to a point when He pulls you through that situation. I use to run from the word but it came to the point that I could not run anymore. I had to face my enemies and pray to God to deliver me from the pain that they caused me and forgive them so I could see in the spirit vision what type of person they could eventually become in the future. Sometimes pride stops us from doing what is right also. We must defeat that spirit and follow Jesus' steps and let Him guide us on how to defeat that stronghold. Jesus gives everyone the opportunity to return home to Him and Jesus just wants us to give our brothers and sisters the same. When you know you truly have love in your heart is when you can forgive and love everyone just like Christ loves us. We must destroy the hate and show more compassion!

Pray

❧

We as God children must realize that our lifeline to God is through Prayer. Thessalonians 5:17 reads, *"Anything that we need and want, he will deliver if it is according to his will."* Praying is not always getting on your knees; you can have a conversation with God while you are driving to work or laying in the bed. You can even write down your prayer in a prayer journal. God wants to hear from us and talk with us like we talk to our own children. He wants to hear what you are struggling with, and He wants us to ask him for help. He may not answer you right away, but he hears our cries. Psalms 18:6 says, *"But in my distress I cried out to the LORD; yes, I prayed to my God for help. He heard me from his sanctuary; my cry to him reached his ears."*

Sometimes when our prayers are not being answered, it's not that it's not in His will. We may have something in our hearts that is hindering us from receiving the blessing that He wants us to have. We all need to ask our Father to reveal anything that we have in our hearts, that would cause us to miss out on our blessings. In my case, forgiveness was a huge issue for me and that was causing me to miss out on most of my blessings or receiving the full potential of them. When I was able to forgive the family member that I discussed earlier, it seemed like the flood gates opened for me. I received all types of blessings that I thought that I could not ever receive. Even though we receive blessings from God, we still will have our problems too, but you can't let that stop you from praying.

Sometimes I find myself praying and not even realizing it. I will wake up in the middle of the night and find myself praying while I'm laying down. I just find myself at peace when ever I reach out to God.

I make it a point to start my day with Him and have conversations throughout the day and He is the last one I speak with before I fall asleep. You see, we all make mistakes and I try to make it a point to communicate with God so I will make less mistakes meaning sinning. I always ask Him for forgiveness for the sins that I know I have made and for the sins that I unknowingly have made.

I use to be afraid to pray because I felt that I did not know how to pray. I use to hear people praying using fancy words and terminology. God just wants to hear from you. In Luke 11:2-4 Jesus said, *"This is how you should pray: Father, may your name be kept holy. May your Kingdom come soon. Give us each day the food we need, and forgive us our sins, as we forgive those who sin against us. And don't let us yield to temptation."* When I pray now, I use Luke 11:2-4 as a blue print. I sometimes pray this prayer but when I use my own words, I always start off by recognizing God for who He is and praising Him.

Then the second part of my prayer I confess any sins that I may have committed that day and repent and ask for forgiveness. After I ask for forgiveness, I pray for my family, friends, and my enemies and ask God to bless them. I then ask God to supply my every need and if I have any wants, I ask Him that as well according to His will. After I ask for my wants, and needs, I always thank Him for what He has done in the past, present and future.

God is here for us and nothing can separate us from Him. When Jesus was on the cross, he prayed to God and asked Him to forgive his crucifiers. Now you see that what Jesus did for us was all about forgiveness That we may one day live with Him and have everlasting life in Paradise!

Strategies for Forgiveness

It would be a good idea to create a strategic plan so when the enemy comes at you with thoughts on why you should not forgive, you will have ammunition to defeat the enemy with. Without being prepared, the enemy can attack you from all different angles.

Always put God first by spending time with Him by yourself. Tell Him your most inner thoughts and make sure you are honest with Him.

Make a list of people that you have a hard time forgiving.

When you pray, pray to the Lord to touch your heart and help you to forgive that person.

Pray for that person that hurt you.

Find a scripture in the Bible that will help you deal with that person.

Ask God to forgive that person for mistreating you or others that you care about.

Ask God to reveal to you what you need to change in your life to make you a better person.

Ask God to reveal to you what is stopping you from moving forward with forgiving yourself and others and ask Him for help.

Each day pray for a different person that has offended you.

Closing Words

F orgiveness is the key to complete happiness. You will be at peace and knowing that our Lord Jesus Christ is pleased with you for taking the first step towards him to give you the strength to forgive others and yourself. We all have power in the blood of Christ we just have to tap into it. Jesus loves everyone and if we want to live and be as much like him, we must pray and ask him for strength to help us love like he does.

For knowledge and understanding, it is best that you read this book with the scriptures that was provide. Below are some other scriptures that might be helpful for you depending on your situation.

Travis W. Simmons

Matthews 6:15	Matthews 18:22	1 John 1:9
Luke 23:34	Mark 11:25	Luke 17:4
Romans 1:9	Psalms 32:6	Daniel 6:13

About the Author

Travis W. Simmons was born in Gastonia North Carolina where he was brought up in the house of the Lord. His Father was the minister of music at their home church for over 20 plus years. His Mother along with other family members made sure that they attended church regularly.

Travis was born again at the age of eleven. He had gone to revival with his grandmother one evening which changed his life. He confessed his sins and asked Jesus Christ to be his Lord and Savior. Travis backslid for a season but thank the Lord that he did not give up on him. Travis rededicated his life and has been serving the Lord since.

Along with his wife Juanita and Children, Travis R. Simmons, Jaquan C. Simmons, Tyler C. Simmons, and Aliyah M. Simmons, Travis continues to be dedicated to serving Jesus Christ our Lord and Savior. Travis continues to try to help others in need and support his family spiritually.

About the Book

Why should I forgive gives readers feedback on how our Lord Jesus Christ helped Travis overcome some of the tribulations that he had to endure. The book also provides knowledge on how to forgive yourself and others who may have offended you.

Acknowledgements

I first would like to thank my Lord and Savior Jesus Christ for saving my life and allowing me to communicate to all by using me to write this book. I would like to thank my Loving wife Juanita Simmons for supporting me and my vision. Thanks to my Pastor Dr. Kimberly Moore for delivering the word of God every week and special thanks to Ronald Simmons, Michael Mauney, Cornell Mauney, Rufus Friday, and Fred Wallace for being great mentors in my life. Thank you to all my Family for your support.

CPSIA information can be obtained
at www.ICGtesting.com
Printed in the USA
LVHW072016180520
655943LV00023B/347

9 781631 291876